Better Homes and Gardens®

Fast-Fixin' Meat Recipes

Our seal assures you that every recipe in *Fast-Fixin' Meat Recipes*
has been tested in the Better Homes and Gardens® Test Kitchen.
This means that each recipe is practical and reliable,
and meets our high standards of taste appeal.

BETTER HOMES AND GARDENS® BOOKS

Editor: Gerald M. Knox
Art Director: Ernest Shelton
Managing Editor: David A. Kirchner
Editorial Project Managers: James D. Blume, Marsha Jahns,
    Rosanne Weber Mattson, Mary Helen Schiltz

Department Head, Cook Books: Sharyl Heiken
Associate Department Heads: Sandra Granseth,
    Rosemary C. Hutchinson, Elizabeth Woolever
Senior Food Editors: Julia Malloy, Marcia Stanley,
    Joyce Trollope
Associate Food Editors: Linda Henry, Mary Major,
    Diana McMillen, Mary Jo Plutt, Martha Schiel,
    Linda Foley Woodrum
Test Kitchen: Director, Sharon Stilwell; Photo Studio Director,
    Janet Herwig; Home Economists: Jean Brekke, Kay Cargill,
    Marilyn Cornelius, Jennifer Darling, Maryellyn Krantz,
    Lynelle Munn, Dianna Nolin, Marge Steenson

Associate Art Directors: Linda Ford Vermie, Neoma Thomas,
    Randall Yontz
Assistant Art Directors: Lynda Haupert, Harijs Priekulis,
    Tom Wegner
Graphic Designers: Mike Burns, Brian Wignall
Art Production: Director, John Berg; Associate, Joe Heuer;
    Office Manager, Michaela Lester

President, Book Group: Fred Stines
Vice President, General Manager: Jeramy Lanigan
Vice President, Retail Marketing: Jamie L. Martin
Vice President, Administrative Services: Rick Rundall

BETTER HOMES AND GARDENS® MAGAZINE
President, Magazine Group: James A. Autry
Vice President, Editorial Director: Doris Eby
Executive Director, Editorial Services: Duane L. Gregg
Food and Nutrition Editor: Nancy Byal

MEREDITH CORPORATE OFFICERS
Chairman of the Board: E.T. Meredith III
President: Robert A. Burnett
Executive Vice President: Jack D. Rehm

FAST-FIXIN' MEAT RECIPES

Editor: Mary Major
Editorial Project Manager: Mary Helen Schiltz
Contributing Graphic Designer: Shelley Caldwell
Electronic Text Processor: Paula Forest
Food Stylists: Kathleen E. German, Janet Herwig
Contributing Photographers: Wm. Hopkins, Scott Little

On the cover: *Pork Medaillons with Apricots*
(see recipe, page 75)

Contents

MEET THE MEATS

After a day packed with activity, the last thing you need to think about is what to cook for dinner. We're here to help with stress-free beef, pork, lamb, and veal entrées that you can turn out in 45 minutes or less.

When it comes to nutrition, you'll find meat hard to beat. It's one of our best sources of protein, B vitamins, and iron. And today, it's lower in calories, fat, and cholesterol than ever before.

Turn these pages for recipes using quick-to-cook steaks, chops, and ground meats; fully cooked ham and sausage; and deli meats. Choose one to fix tonight.

Lamb Chops with Walnut Sauce
Ready in 20 minutes
(see recipe, page 24)

Beef with Marsala
Ready in 25 minutes
(see recipe, page 75)

Ham with Cucumber Sauce
Ready in 10 minutes
(see recipe, page 42)

Veggie-Stuffed Steak

Total Time: 25 minutes

2 tablespoons margarine *or* butter
1 small potato, peeled and shredded
1 small carrot, shredded
1 green onion, chopped
¼ cup grated Parmesan cheese

● In a medium saucepan melt the margarine or butter. Add potato, carrot, and onion. Cook till tender, stirring occasionally. Remove from heat. Stir in Parmesan cheese. Cool slightly.

1 1½- to 2-pound beef top loin steak, cut 1 to 1½ inches thick

● Meanwhile, cut the steak in half crosswise. Cut a large slit horizontally in each half to form a pocket. Spoon the vegetable mixture into the pocket. Secure opening with wooden skewers or toothpicks. Season with salt and pepper.

● Place steaks on the unheated rack of a broiler pan. Broil 4 to 5 inches from heat for 6 minutes. Turn steaks and broil to desired doneness (allow 6 to 8 minutes for medium). Remove skewers or toothpicks. Cut into serving-size pieces. Makes 4 servings.

A vegetable trio, accompanied by grated Parmesan cheese, performs flavorfully in this broiled steak.

Tangy Ham Slice

Total Time: 30 minutes

⅓ cup currant jelly
2 tablespoons lemon juice
¼ teaspoon ground cinnamon

● Preheat the broiler. Meanwhile, for sauce, in a small saucepan combine currant jelly, lemon juice, and cinnamon. Cook over low heat till jelly is melted.

Currant jelly jazzed up with cinnamon and lemon juice makes an easy sauce for this ham slice.

1 2-pound fully cooked ham slice, cut 1 inch thick
Lemon slices (optional)

● Place the ham slice on the unheated rack of a broiler pan. Broil 3 to 4 inches from heat for 7 minutes. Brush with sauce. Turn ham slice. Broil for 6 minutes. Brush with additional sauce. Broil for 1 to 3 minutes more or till ham is heated through. Brush with remaining sauce. Garnish with lemon slices, if desired. Makes 8 servings.

Honey-Mustard Pork Chops

Total Time: 30 minutes

2 tablespoons sliced green onion
2 tablespoons orange juice
1 tablespoon honey
1 teaspoon prepared mustard
¼ teaspoon salt
⅛ teaspoon pepper

● Preheat the broiler. Meanwhile, for sauce, in a small bowl mix together green onion, orange juice, honey, mustard, salt, and pepper. Set aside.

The honey and mustard combination gives the sauce an Oriental sweet-sour flavor.

4 pork loin chops, cut ¾ inch thick

● Place the pork chops on the unheated rack of a broiler pan. Broil chops 4 to 5 inches from heat for 8 minutes. Brush chops with sauce. Turn chops. Broil for 5 minutes more. Brush with the remaining sauce. Broil 2 to 4 minutes more or till meat is no longer pink. Makes 4 servings.

Peppery Pork Chops

Total Time: 30 minutes

1 tablespoon paprika
1 teaspoon garlic salt
½ teaspoon pepper
4 pork loin chops, cut
   ¾ inch thick

● In a small mixing bowl combine paprika, garlic salt, and pepper. Mix well. Rub each chop with paprika mixture.

½ cup dairy sour cream

● Place the pork chops on the unheated rack of a broiler pan. Broil chops 4 to 5 inches from the heat for 8 minutes. Turn chops and broil for 7 to 9 minutes more or till the meat is no longer pink. Serve with sour cream. Makes 4 servings.

Our Test Kitchen recommends ¾-inch-thick pork chops for broiling. They're thick enough to stay juicy, but thin enough to cook quickly.

Steak with Tarragon Butter

Total Time: 30 minutes

¼ cup margarine *or* butter,
   softened
1 clove garlic, minced
1 teaspoon lemon juice
½ teaspoon dried tarragon,
   crushed

● Preheat the broiler. Stir together margarine or butter, garlic, lemon juice, and tarragon. Chill butter mixture while preparing steaks.

2 1-pound beef porterhouse,
   T-bone, *or* sirloin
   steaks, cut 1½ inches
   thick

● Without cutting into the meat, slash fat edges at 1-inch intervals. Place steaks on the unheated rack of a broiler pan.
   Broil steaks 3 to 4 inches from heat for 10 minutes (see photo, right). Turn steaks. Broil to desired doneness (allow 8 to 10 minutes more for medium). Cut steaks into serving-size pieces. Serve with the butter mixture. Makes 6 servings.

Whether you like your steak rare, medium, or well-done, keep it juicy by cooking it the specified distance from the heat. Place the meat on the rack in the broiler pan. Measure the distance from the top of the meat to the heating element. Adjust the oven racks as necessary.

Lamb and Fruit Kabobs

Total Time: 30 minutes

1 medium apple
1 medium banana
  Lemon juice
1 pound boneless lamb, cut into 1-inch cubes

● Preheat the broiler. Remove core from apple. Cut into thick wedges. Cut the banana into 1-inch pieces. Brush the fruit with lemon juice. Thread fruit on four 8- or 9-inch skewers. Thread meat on 4 additional skewers.

Jump the gun when selecting the banana. One that's not quite ripe will have a better color and texture after broiling.

½ of a 6-ounce can (⅓ cup) frozen apple juice concentrate
2 teaspoons lemon juice
½ teaspoon instant beef bouillon granules
¼ teaspoon ground cloves

● For sauce, in a small saucepan mix together apple juice concentrate, lemon juice, bouillon granules, and cloves. Cook till mixture boils. Remove from heat.

● Place meat kabobs on the unheated rack of a broiler pan. Broil 3 to 4 inches from the heat for 5 minutes. Brush with sauce. Turn kabobs over. Add fruit kabobs to broiler pan. Brush meat and fruit with sauce. Broil to desired doneness (allow 6 to 8 minutes for medium), brushing occasionally with sauce. Makes 4 servings.

Peanutty Pork Kabobs

Total Time: 40 minutes

3 tablespoons soy sauce
2 tablespoons peanut butter
2 tablespoons lemon juice
2 tablespoons cooking oil
½ teaspoon ground coriander
⅛ teaspoon onion powder
⅛ teaspoon ground red pepper

● Preheat the broiler. Meanwhile, for sauce, in a medium mixing bowl combine soy sauce, peanut butter, lemon juice, cooking oil, coriander, onion powder, and red pepper. Set aside.

Let your store do the work—shop for pork already cut into cubes. If you can't find it, or you prefer to cut your own, choose pork loin.

1 pound lean boneless pork, cut into 1-inch cubes
1 medium zucchini, cut into ¼-inch-thick slices
12 large mushroom caps

● For the kabobs, on four 12- or 14-inch skewers alternately thread pork cubes, zucchini, and mushrooms.

  Hot cooked rice

● Place kabobs on the unheated rack of a broiler pan. Brush with sauce. Broil 3 to 4 inches from the heat for 8 minutes. Turn kabobs. Brush with sauce. Broil for 7 to 8 minutes more or till meat is no longer pink. Brush with sauce. Serve with rice. Makes 4 servings.

Sausage-Potato Kabobs

Total Time: 25 minutes

¼ cup margarine *or* butter
2 tablespoons lemon juice
½ teaspoon garlic powder
½ teaspoon dried oregano, crushed

● Preheat the broiler. In a small saucepan combine margarine or butter, lemon juice, garlic powder, and oregano. Cook over low heat till margarine is melted. Remove from heat. Set aside.

If your skewers are shorter than 14 inches, just use more of them. Cook the shorter kabobs the same as you would the longer ones.

1 pound fully cooked Polish sausage, bratwurst, *or* knockwurst
1 medium yellow summer squash *or* zucchini, cut into ½-inch-thick slices
1 large sweet red or green pepper, cut into 1-inch pieces
1 16-ounce can whole white potatoes, drained

● Cut sausage into 2-inch pieces. On four 14- or 15-inch-long skewers alternately thread sausage, squash, red or green pepper, and potatoes. Place kabobs on the unheated rack of a broiler pan. Brush kabobs with lemon mixture.

● Broil kabobs 3 to 4 inches from the heat for 5 minutes. Turn kabobs. Brush with remaining lemon mixture. Broil for 5 to 7 minutes more or till vegetables are crisp-tender and sausage is heated through. Makes 4 servings.

Mustard Sauce

Chili-Barbecue Sauce

Mushroom Wine Sauce

Total Time: 15 minutes

1	cup sliced fresh mushrooms
1	small onion, chopped
2	tablespoons margarine *or* butter

● In a medium saucepan cook mushrooms and onion in margarine or butter about 5 minutes or till vegetables are tender.

½	cup water
½	cup dry red wine
1	tablespoon cornstarch
1	teaspoon instant beef bouillon granules
1	tablespoon snipped parsley

● Stir in water, wine, cornstarch, and bouillon granules. Cook and stir till thickened and bubbly. Cook and stir for 2 minutes more. Stir in parsley. Serve sauce over broiled beef, pork, lamb, or veal. Store any leftover sauce in a covered container in the refrigerator up to 2 weeks. Makes 1⅓ cups.

Dress up steaks or chops with one of these simple full-flavored sauces.

Chili-Barbecue Sauce

Total Time: 5 minutes

1	8-ounce can tomato sauce
1	4-ounce can diced green chili peppers, drained
1	tablespoon steak sauce
2	teaspoons chili powder
¼	teaspoon ground cumin
⅛	teaspoon garlic powder

● In a small saucepan combine tomato sauce, chili peppers, steak sauce, chili powder, cumin, and garlic powder. Bring to boiling. Reduce heat. Cover and simmer 5 minutes.
　Brush onto beef, pork, lamb, or veal during last half of broiling. Pass additional sauce, if desired. Store leftover sauce in covered container in refrigerator up to 2 weeks. Makes 1¼ cups.

Chili powder, cumin, and chili peppers give this barbecue sauce a Mexican flavor.

Mushroom Wine Sauce

Mustard Sauce

Total Time: 5 minutes

½ of an 8-ounce container dairy sour cream
2 tablespoons Dijon-style mustard
¼ teaspoon dried tarragon, crushed

● In a small mixing bowl combine sour cream, mustard, and tarragon. Mix well. Serve over broiled beef, pork, lamb, or veal. Store any leftover sauce in a covered container in the refrigerator up to 1 week. Makes about ⅔ cup.

Two sauces in one, this fast-fixin' sauce for broiled meats doubles as a sandwich spread. Use it in place of mayonnaise on a sandwich.

Broiler Tips

Follow these directions for juicy broiled meats. Preheat the broiler. Adjust the racks so the meat is the specified distance from the heat. Place the meat on the unheated rack of the broiler pan. Broil for half the time. Turn the meat and broil till done.

MEAT	COOKING TIME	INCHES FROM HEAT
Steak, 1½ inches thick	18 to 20 minutes	3 to 4 inches
Lamb chops, ¾ inch thick	10 to 12 minutes	3 to 4 inches
Pork chops, ¾ inch thick	15 to 17 minutes	4 to 5 inches
Ham slice, 1 inch thick	15 to 17 minutes	3 to 4 inches

Lamb Chops With Plum Sauce

Total Time: 20 minutes

½ cup plum jelly
2 green onions, sliced
2 tablespoons dry sherry
2 tablespoons soy sauce
1 tablespoon cornstarch
1 tablespoon lemon juice

● Preheat the broiler. For sauce, in a small saucepan combine jelly, green onions, sherry, soy sauce, cornstarch, and lemon juice. Cook and stir till thickened and bubbly. Cook and stir for 1 to 2 minutes more. Remove from heat.

Take a tip from our Test Kitchen: Turn chops with tongs instead of a fork. A fork will pierce the meat, allowing the juices to escape and causing the meat to dry out.

8 lamb rib *or* loin chops *or*
4 leg sirloin chops, cut
¾ inch thick

● Slash the fat edges of chops in several places. Place chops on the unheated rack of a broiler pan. Brush with some of the sauce. Broil chops 3 to 4 inches from the heat for 5 minutes. Turn chops. Brush with additional sauce. Broil to desired doneness (allow 5 to 7 minutes for medium). Pass remaining sauce. Makes 4 servings.

Herbed Lamb Chops and Tomatoes

Total Time: 25 minutes

2 tablespoons cooking oil 1 teaspoon dried rosemary, crushed ¼ teaspoon garlic salt ¼ teaspoon dried oregano, crushed ¼ teaspoon pepper	● Preheat the broiler. In a small mixing bowl combine cooking oil, rosemary, garlic salt, oregano, and pepper.
8 lamb rib *or* loin chops *or* 4 leg sirloin chops, cut ¾ inch thick	● Slash the fat edges of chops in several places. Place chops on the unheated rack of a broiler pan. Brush with herb mixture. Broil chops 3 to 4 inches from the heat for 5 minutes.
2 large tomatoes 1 tablespoon grated Parmesan cheese	● Meanwhile, cut tomatoes in half crosswise. Sprinkle each half with Parmesan cheese. Turn chops. Brush with remaining herb mixture. Add tomato halves to broiler pan. Broil till meat is desired doneness (allow 5 to 7 minutes for medium). Makes 4 servings.

Once upon a time lamb lovers cooked their chops till well done. Today, many find chops more tender and juicy cooked just to medium.

Mushroom-Topped Beef Patties

SUPER FAST

Total Time: 20 minutes

1 beaten egg 2 tablespoons milk ¼ cup fine dry bread crumbs ¼ teaspoon salt ⅛ teaspoon pepper 1 pound ground beef *or* ground lamb	● In a medium mixing bowl combine egg and milk. Stir in bread crumbs, salt, and pepper. Add ground meat and mix well. Shape meat mixture into four ¾-inch-thick patties. 　Place patties on the unheated rack of a broiler pan. Broil 3 to 4 inches from the heat for 6 minutes. Turn patties over, Broil 6 to 8 minutes more or till meat is no longer pink.
¼ of an 8-ounce container soft-style cream cheese 2 tablespoons crumbled blue cheese 1 2½-ounce jar sliced mushrooms, drained 1 tablespoon snipped chives	● Meanwhile, in a small mixing bowl combine cream cheese and blue cheese. Stir in mushrooms. Spread mushroom mixture over patties. Broil for 2 to 3 minutes more or till topping is hot. Sprinkle with chives. Makes 4 servings.

For a super-easy recipe, omit the chives and use cream cheese with chives and onion in place of the plain cream cheese.

SUPER FAST

Orange-Curried Lamb

Total Time: 20 minutes

¾	**pound boneless lamb**
½	**cup chicken broth**
½	**cup orange juice**
1	**tablespoon cornstarch**
1	**tablespoon curry powder**
⅛	**teaspoon salt**
⅛	**teaspoon onion powder**

● Cut the lamb on the bias into thin bite-size strips. For sauce, stir together chicken broth, orange juice, cornstarch, curry powder, salt, and onion powder. Set aside.

In a hurry? Try our curry. Stir-fried lamb strips, pea pods, and tomatoes cook in a flash.

1	**tablespoon cooking oil**

● Preheat a wok or 12-inch skillet over high heat. Add the cooking oil. (Add more oil as necessary during cooking.) Add lamb to wok or skillet. Stir-fry about 3 minutes or till lamb is no longer pink. Push from center of wok.

1	**6-ounce package frozen pea pods**
1	**medium tomato, cut into thin wedges**
½	**cup peanuts**
½	**cup raisins**
	Hot cooked couscous *or* rice

● Stir sauce. Add sauce to the center of the wok or skillet. Cook and stir till thickened and bubbly. Stir meat into sauce. Stir in pea pods, tomato, peanuts, and raisins. Cook about 2 minutes more or till heated through. Serve over couscous or rice. Makes 4 servings.

Pork and Green Bean Stir-Fry

SUPER FAST

Total Time: 20 minutes

1 pound boneless pork
2 tablespoons soy sauce
2 tablespoons rice wine vinegar *or* red wine vinegar
½ teaspoon crushed red pepper
¼ teaspoon ground ginger

● Cut pork on the bias into thin bite-size strips. For sauce, stir together soy sauce, vinegar, crushed red pepper, and ginger. Set aside.

When minutes count, buy boneless pork loin for this recipe. This meat is so lean that you can quickly cut it into strips.

1 9-ounce package frozen French-style green beans
1 tablespoon cooking oil
1 clove garlic, minced, *or* ½ teaspoon bottled minced garlic

● Run hot water over green beans in colander to thaw. Pat dry with paper towels. Preheat a wok or large skillet over high heat. Add cooking oil. (Add more oil as necessary during cooking.) Add green beans and garlic. Stir-fry for 1½ minutes. Remove beans from wok.

● Add half of the pork to hot wok or skillet. Stir-fry about 3 minutes or till no longer pink. Remove pork. Repeat with remaining pork. Return all the pork and green beans to wok. Add sauce. Toss to coat. Makes 4 servings.

Lemon-Sauced Pork

Total Time: 20 minutes

¾ **pound boneless pork**
½ **cup cold water**
¼ **cup dry white wine**
2 **tablespoons soy sauce**
1 **tablespoon cornstarch**
1 **teaspoon instant chicken bouillon granules**
½ **teaspoon finely shredded lemon peel**

● Cut pork on the bias into thin bite-size strips. For sauce, stir together water, wine, soy sauce, cornstarch, bouillon granules, and lemon peel. Set aside.

A little lemon peel provides the fresh lemon flavor in this stir-fry dish.

1 **10-ounce package frozen cut asparagus**
1 **tablespoon cooking oil**
1 **small onion, thinly sliced**
1 **8-ounce can sliced water chestnuts, drained**

● Run water over frozen asparagus to thaw (see photo, below). Pat dry with paper towels. Preheat a wok or large skillet over high heat. Add cooking oil. (Add more oil as necessary during cooking.) Add asparagus and onion. Stir-fry about 3 minutes or till crisp-tender. Remove vegetables.
   Add pork to hot wok. Stir-fry about 3 minutes or till no longer pink. Return vegetables to wok. Stir in water chestnuts. Push from center of the wok.

Hot cooked rice

● Stir sauce. Add to center of wok. Cook and stir till thickened and bubbly. Cook and stir for 2 minutes more. Serve over rice. Makes 4 servings.

To quick-thaw frozen vegetables, place the frozen vegetables in a colander. Run hot tap water over the vegetables till thawed. Drain well. For stir-frying, pat the vegetables dry with paper towels to prevent spattering.

Beef and Cauliflower Stir-Fry

Total Time: 25 minutes

¾ **pound beef top round
   steak**
⅓ **cup cold water**
⅓ **cup dry red wine**
2 **teaspoons cornstarch**
¼ **teaspoon dried thyme,
   crushed**
⅛ **teaspoon salt**

● Cut beef on the bias into thin bite-size strips. For sauce, stir together water, wine, cornstarch, thyme, and salt.

**Trapped in a time-bind?
Free yourself with this
thyme-flavored dish.**

1 **tablespoon cooking oil**
½ **of a medium head
   cauliflower, broken into
   flowerets and sliced
   (about 2 cups)**
3 **medium carrots, thinly
   bias sliced (1½ cups)**

● Preheat a wok or 12-inch skillet over high heat. Add cooking oil to the wok or skillet. (Add more oil as necessary during cooking.) Add cauliflower and carrots. Stir-fry for 4 to 5 minutes or till vegetables are crisp-tender. Remove vegetables. Add beef. Stir-fry for 2 to 3 minutes or till beef is no longer pink. Push beef from the center of wok.

**Hot cooked rice *or*
   noodles**
1 **green onion, sliced**

● Stir sauce. Add to center of wok. Cook and stir till thickened and bubbly. Cook and stir 2 minutes more. Return vegetables to wok. Stir ingredients together. Serve over rice or noodles. Sprinkle with green onion. Serves 4.

Gingered Beef and Vegetables

Total Time: 25 minutes

1 pound beef top round steak *or* lean boneless pork 2 tablespoons cold water 2 tablespoons soy sauce 2 tablespoons dry sherry 1 teaspoon cornstarch ¼ teaspoon ground ginger ⅛ teaspoon garlic powder	● Cut the meat on the bias into thin bite-size strips. For sauce, stir together water, soy sauce, sherry, cornstarch, ginger, and garlic powder. Set aside.
3 cups loose-pack frozen mixed broccoli, cauliflower, and carrots 1 tablespoon cooking oil	● Cut any large pieces of vegetables in half. Preheat a wok or 12-inch skillet over high heat. Add cooking oil. (Add more oil as necessary during cooking.) Add vegetables. Stir-fry about 4 minutes or till crisp-tender. Remove vegetables from the wok. Add *half* of the meat to the wok. Stir-fry for 2 to 3 minutes or till meat is no longer pink. Remove meat from the wok. Stir-fry remaining meat for 2 to 3 minutes. Return all the meat and the vegetables to the wok. Push meat and vegetables from the center of the wok.
Hot cooked rice	● Stir the sauce. Add sauce to the center of the wok. Cook and stir till thickened and bubbly. Cook and stir for 2 minutes more. Stir ingredients together. Serve with hot rice. Serves 4.

To minimize chopping, we added frozen vegetables to this soy- and ginger-flavored dish.

Easy Ground Beef Stir-Fry

SUPER FAST

Total Time: 15 minutes

½ cup cold water
3 tablespoons soy sauce
1 tablespoon cornstarch
½ teaspoon ground ginger
⅛ teaspoon garlic powder

● For sauce, stir together cold water, soy sauce, cornstarch, ginger, and garlic powder. Set aside.

1 10-ounce package frozen cut broccoli
1 tablespoon cooking oil

● Run water over broccoli to thaw. Pat dry with paper towels. Preheat a wok or large skillet over high heat. Add cooking oil. (Add more oil if necessary during cooking.) Stir-fry broccoli for 2 to 3 minutes or till crisp-tender. Remove broccoli from the wok.

1 pound lean ground beef
1 8-ounce can sliced water chestnuts, drained

● Crumble *half* of the ground beef into the hot wok or skillet. Stir-fry about 2 minutes or till beef loses its pink color. Remove beef. Stir-fry remaining beef about 2 minutes. Drain off fat. Return all beef and broccoli to the wok. Stir in water chestnuts. Push from the center of the wok or skillet.

Hot cooked rice

● Stir the sauce. Add sauce to the center of the wok. Cook and stir till thickened and bubbly. Cook and stir for 2 minutes more. Serve with hot cooked rice. Makes 4 servings.

Put your knife away. Ground beef, frozen cut broccoli, and canned sliced water chestnuts make this a chop-free stir-fry dish.

Pork Chow Mein

Total Time: 25 minutes

¾ **pound boneless pork**
¾ **cup orange juice**
2 **tablespoons soy sauce**
1 **tablespoon cornstarch**
¼ **teaspoon ground ginger**
⅛ **teaspoon garlic powder**

● Cut pork on the bias into thin bite-size strips. For sauce, combine orange juice, soy sauce, cornstarch, ginger, and garlic powder. Set aside.

Orange juice and ginger zip up the flavor of this stir-fry standby.

1 **tablespoon cooking oil**
2 **medium carrots, thinly bias-sliced**

● Preheat a wok or a large skillet over high heat. Add cooking oil to the hot wok (add more oil as necessary during cooking). Add carrots. Cook and stir about 4 minutes or till crisp-tender. Remove carrots. Add the pork. Cook and stir about 3 minutes or till no longer pink. Push from the center of the wok.

1 **6-ounce package frozen pea pods**
Chow mein noodles, heated

● Stir sauce. Add to the center of wok. Cook and stir till thickened and bubbly. Cook and stir for 1 minute more. Return carrots to wok. Stir in pea pods. Cover and cook 1 minute. Serve over warm chow mein noodles. Makes 4 servings.

Stay a Chop Ahead

Meat and vegetables stir-fry in only a few minutes, but slicing and chopping take some preparation time. To speed things up, invest in good quality knives and keep them sharp. And on some days, you may find it easier to prepare the meat and vegetables the night before or earlier in the day. Just store them separately in airtight containers in the refrigerator till mealtime.

Many grocery stores slice and package beef, pork, and lamb strips especially for stir-frying. Some stores also sell prechopped fresh vegetables. Keep an eye out for these timesaving products.

Veal with Vegetables

Total Time: 20 minutes

2 tablespoons cooking oil 1 medium green pepper, cut into 1-inch pieces 1 medium onion, sliced ¼ teaspoon bottled minced garlic *or* dash garlic powder* 4 veal cubed steaks	● In a 12-inch skillet heat cooking oil. Add green pepper, onion, and minced garlic. Cook about 2 minutes or till vegetables are tender. Remove vegetables with a slotted spoon. Add more oil to the skillet, if necessary. Cook veal in hot oil for 4 to 5 minutes or till meat is no longer pink, turning once.
2 medium tomatoes, cut into wedges 1 ounce sliced pepperoni	● Return cooked vegetables to the skillet. Stir in tomatoes and pepperoni. Cover and cook for 1 to 2 minutes or till heated through.
1 tablespoon lemon juice	● Transfer veal and vegetables to a serving platter. Stir lemon juice into pan juices. Spoon the juices over veal and vegetables. Makes 4 servings. ***Note:** If using garlic powder, add with tomatoes and pepperoni.

Fresh tomatoes, green pepper, pepperoni, and garlic make an easy and flavorful sauce for this Italian-style dish.

Lamb Chops With Walnut Sauce

Total Time: 20 minutes

8 lamb rib *or* loin chops, cut 1 inch thick (about 2 pounds total) 3 tablespoons margarine *or* butter	● Trim excess fat from chops. In a large skillet melt margarine or butter. Add chops and cook over medium heat for 4 minutes. Turn chops. Cook to desired doneness (allow 4 to 6 minutes for medium). Season with salt and pepper. 　Transfer lamb chops to a serving platter and keep warm. Drain skillet, reserving 1 tablespoon drippings.
⅓ cup chopped walnuts ¼ cup orange juice 2 tablespoons currant jelly *or* orange marmalade	● For sauce, add walnuts to drippings in skillet. Cook for 1 to 2 minutes or till brown, stirring constantly. Stir in orange juice, and jelly or marmalade. Bring to boiling. Cook, stirring constantly, for 1 to 2 minutes or till sauce is slightly thickened. Spoon sauce over chops. Makes 4 servings.

Pictured on pages 4 and 5.

Grocery stores label lamb rib chops with a variety of names. You may find them called French chops, French lamb chops, or rib kabobs.

Veal with Vegetables

Beef with Cream Gravy

Total Time: 30 minutes

1½ **pounds beef round steak**	● Cut the steak into 6 serving-size pieces. Place each piece of steak between 2 sheets of clear plastic wrap. Pound to ¼-inch thickness. Remove plastic wrap.
2 **tablespoons margarine** *or* **butter** **Salt** **Pepper**	● In a 12-inch heavy skillet melt margarine or butter. Add half of the steak. Cook over medium-high heat about 4 minutes or till no pink remains, turning once. Remove from skillet. Repeat with remaining steak. Season with salt and pepper. Transfer steak to a serving platter. Cover to keep warm.
¾ **cup beef broth** 1 **4-ounce can sliced mushrooms, drained** ⅓ **cup light cream** *or* **milk** 2 **tablespoons all-purpose flour**	● For gravy, in same skillet combine beef broth and mushrooms. In a screw-top jar combine cream or milk, and flour. Cover and shake well. Add to liquid in skillet. Cook and stir till thickened and bubbly. Cook and stir for 1 minute more. Serve gravy over steak. Makes 6 servings.

Round steak usually needs an hour or more of simmering. We reduced that time by pounding the steak to tenderize it.

SUPER FAST

Cheese-Stuffed Beef Rolls

Total Time: 20 minutes

½ **of a 4-ounce container whipped cream cheese** 1 **to 2 teaspoons prepared horseradish** 4 **beef cubed steaks (about 4 ounces each)** 4 **green onions**	● Combine cream cheese and horseradish. Spread each steak with cream cheese mixture. Place a green onion at the wide end of each steak. Roll up steak around green onion (see photo, right). Secure with wooden toothpick.
1 **tablespoon cooking oil**	● Preheat a large skillet over medium-high heat. Add oil. Cook beef rolls in hot oil for 8 to 10 minutes or till no pink remains. Remove beef rolls from skillet. Keep warm. Drain fat from skillet.
1 **8-ounce can tomato sauce** 1 **2-ounce can chopped mushrooms, drained** ½ **teaspoon dried marjoram, crushed** **Hot cooked noodles**	● For sauce, in the same skillet combine tomato sauce, mushrooms, and marjoram. Cook about 1 minute or till heated through. Serve beef rolls over noodles and top with sauce. Serves 4.

Place the green onion at the wide end of the steak. Wrap the steak around the green onion, then secure with a wooden toothpick. Remove the toothpicks before serving.

Beefy Tomato-Rice Dinner

Total Time: 30 minutes

1 pound ground beef	● In a large saucepan cook ground beef till brown. Drain off fat.
1 16-ounce can tomatoes, cut up 1 9-ounce package frozen cut green beans 1 8-ounce can tomato sauce 1 cup water 1 6-ounce package regular curry-flavored rice mix with raisins and almonds	● Stir in *undrained* tomatoes, green beans, tomato sauce, water, and rice and seasoning packet. Bring to boiling. Reduce heat. Cover and simmer about 25 minutes or till beans are crisp-tender and rice is tender. Sprinkle with almonds from rice mix. Makes 4 servings.

Once you assemble this one-dish meal, let it simmer away while you put your feet up and relax.

Sauerbraten Pork Steaks

SUPER FAST

Total Time: 20 minutes

1 tablespoon cooking oil 4 pork *or* beef cubed steaks	● Heat a large skillet over high heat. Add cooking oil to skillet. Cook steaks in hot oil about 8 minutes or till meat is no longer pink, turning once. Remove steaks and keep warm. Drain fat from skillet.
¾ cup chicken broth ¼ cup finely chopped celery 1 tablespoon brown sugar 1 tablespoon vinegar 1 teaspoon prepared mustard ¼ teaspoon salt Dash pepper 2 tablespoons crushed gingersnaps (2 cookies) Hot cooked noodles	● In the same skillet stir together chicken broth, celery, brown sugar, vinegar, mustard, salt, and pepper. Stir in gingersnaps. Cook and stir till mixture is thick and bubbly. Serve meat and sauce over hot cooked noodles. Serves 4.

We borrowed the flavor from the traditional pot roast of Germany for these cubed steaks.

Pork Chops With Garlic-Ginger Sauce

Total Time: 25 minutes

4 pork loin chops, cut
  ½ inch thick
1 tablespoon cooking oil

● Trim excess fat from chops. Heat oil in a 12-inch skillet. Add chops to hot oil. Cook over medium heat about 8 minutes or till brown on both sides, turning once.

½ cup chicken broth
2 green onions, cut into
  1½-inch pieces
1 teaspoon bottled minced
  garlic *or* ¼ teaspoon
  garlic powder
¼ teaspoon ground ginger
2 tablespoons cold water
2 teaspoons cornstarch

● Add chicken broth, green onion, minced garlic or garlic powder, and ginger to skillet. Bring to boiling. Reduce heat. Cover and simmer about 8 minutes or till chops are tender and no pink remains. Transfer chops to a serving platter. Keep warm.
　　Combine water and cornstarch. Stir into broth mixture in skillet. Cook and stir till thickened and bubbly. Cook and stir for 2 minutes more. Spoon sauce over pork chops. Makes 4 servings.

Calling all garlic lovers. This recipe's sure to please. For a milder garlic flavor, use ½ teaspoon bottled minced garlic or ⅛ teaspoon garlic powder.

Pork with Cream Sauce

Total Time: 25 minutes

2 tablespoons margarine *or*
  butter
4 pork cubed steaks

● In a 12-inch skillet melt margarine or butter. Add pork. Cook for 5 minutes. Turn pork over. Cook for 6 to 8 minutes more or till meat is no longer pink. Season to taste with salt and pepper. Remove pork from skillet. Keep warm.

1 small onion, sliced
1 2½-ounce jar sliced
  mushrooms, drained
½ of an 8-ounce carton dairy
  sour cream
2 tablespoons milk
¼ teaspoon dried tarragon,
  crushed
  Dash pepper

● For sauce, add onion and mushrooms to drippings in the skillet. Cook about 5 minutes or till onion is tender. Reduce heat to low. Stir in sour cream, milk, tarragon, and pepper. Cook, stirring constantly, about 2 minutes or till heated through. *Do not boil.* Serve sauce over pork. Makes 4 servings.

To be the fastest cook on the block, use a 12-inch skillet and cook all the steaks at once. If your skillet is smaller, cook two steaks at a time.

Butterfly Pork Chops with Apple Rings

Total Time: 25 minutes

4 pork loin butterfly chops, cut ½ inch thick **2 tablespoons margarine *or* butter**	● Trim excess fat from chops. Season chops with pepper. In a large skillet melt margarine or butter. Add chops to skillet. Cook over medium heat about 5 minutes or till brown, turning once.
1 6-ounce can (⅔ cup) apple juice **2 tablespoons raisins** **½ teaspoon instant chicken bouillon granules** **Dash ground cinnamon** **Dash ground cloves** **2 medium apples, cored and cut into rings**	● Add apple juice, raisins, bouillon granules, cinnamon, and cloves. Bring to boiling. Reduce heat. Cover and simmer 5 minutes. Add apple rings. Simmer about 5 minutes more or till pork is no longer pink. Transfer chops and apples to a serving platter. Keep warm.
1 tablespoon cold water **2 teaspoons cornstarch**	● Combine water and cornstarch. Stir into juices in the skillet. Cook and stir till thickened and bubbly. Cook and stir for 2 minutes more. Spoon sauce over chops and apple rings. Makes 4 servings.

You won't have a bone to pick with these chops. Boneless butterfly pork chops are perfect for panfrying because they're so tender.

Sausage and Cabbage

Total Time: 15 minutes

| 1 pound fully cooked Polish sausage *or* other smoked sausage
¼ cup water
1 teaspoon instant chicken bouillon granules | ● In a 12-inch skillet combine sausage, water, and bouillon granules. Cover and cook over medium heat for 5 minutes. |

| 1 small head cabbage
2 cups frozen crinkle-cut carrots | ● Meanwhile, cut cabbage into 4 wedges. Remove core. Coarsely shred wedges. Add cabbage and carrots to the skillet. Cover and cook about 10 minutes or till the vegetables are crisp-tender. |

| ½ cup dairy sour cream
½ teaspoon caraway seed | ● Stir sour cream and caraway seed into cabbage mixture. Cover and cook about 3 minutes or till heated through. *Do not boil.* Makes 4 servings. |

One large sausage link or smaller individual links work equally well for *Sausage and Cabbage.* If you have a large link, cut it into 3- to 4-inch lengths.

Franks and Taters

Total Time: 20 minutes

| ½ of a 24-ounce package (3 cups) frozen hash brown potatoes with onion and peppers
1 9-ounce package frozen French-style green beans
½ cup water | ● In a large skillet combine potatoes, green beans, and water. Cover and cook about 5 minutes or till vegetables are just tender. Drain. |

| 1 16-ounce package frankfurters *or* one 12-ounce package fully cooked smoked sausage links
½ cup milk
1 teaspoon cornstarch
1 cup shredded cheddar cheese (4 ounces) | ● Meanwhile, cut frankfurters or sausage links into 1-inch pieces. Add meat to potato mixture. Combine milk and cornstarch. Stir into skillet. Cook and stir till boiling.
    Stir in half of the cheese. Reduce heat to low. Cover and simmer about 5 minutes or till heated through. Sprinkle with the remaining cheese. Serves 4 to 6. |

Cooking without frozen vegetables can mean long hours in the kitchen. So take advantage of their convenience and try this skillet dinner.

Sausage-Macaroni Skillet

Total Time: 30 minutes

1 8-ounce package brown-and-serve sausage links

● In a large skillet cook sausage for 6 to 8 minutes or till brown, turning to cook evenly on all sides. Remove sausage. Drain fat from skillet.

1 16-ounce can tomatoes, cut up
1 7¼-ounce package macaroni-and-cheese mix
1 cup water
¼ cup chopped onion

● In the same skillet combine *undrained* tomatoes, macaroni from the dinner mix, water, and onion. Bring to boiling; reduce heat. Cover and simmer for 10 to 12 minutes or till macaroni is tender, stirring occasionally.

¼ cup margarine *or* butter
¼ cup milk

● Meanwhile, cut sausage links into thirds. Stir cheese sauce packet from mix, margarine or butter, and milk into macaroni mixture. Stir in sausage and cook about 5 minutes more or till heated through. Makes 4 servings.

Recipes like *Sausage-Macaroni Skillet* can be a lifesaver on days when you're on the run and too busy to plan dinner. Just keep the ingredients on hand and you can serve this tasty one-dish meal in half an hour.

Polish Sausage With Beans

SUPER FAST

Total Time: 15 minutes

8 ounces fully cooked Polish sausage *or* one 8-ounce package frankfurters

● Cut the Polish sausage or frankfurters into 1-inch pieces.

1 8½-ounce can lima beans, drained
1 8-ounce can pork and beans with tomato sauce
1 8-ounce can red kidney beans, drained
¼ cup catsup
1 tablespoon brown sugar
1 tablespoon vinegar
⅛ teaspoon onion powder
Dash dry mustard
Dash bottled hot pepper sauce

● In a medium saucepan combine lima beans, pork and beans, kidney beans, catsup, brown sugar, vinegar, onion powder, dry mustard, and hot pepper sauce. Stir in the sausage. Bring to boiling. Reduce heat. Simmer about 5 minutes or till heated through. Serves 3.

When you're in a tighter-than-usual time crunch, substitute ⅓ cup bottled barbecue sauce for the catsup, brown sugar, and vinegar.

Smoked Chops And Potatoes

SUPER FAST

Total Time: 20 minutes

3 **medium potatoes, sliced (about 1 pound)**
1 **cup loose-pack frozen broccoli, cauliflower, and carrots**

● In a large covered skillet cook potatoes and frozen vegetables in enough boiling water to cover for 6 to 8 minutes or till potatoes and vegetables are tender. Drain in colander.

4 **smoked pork chops, cut ½ to ¾ inch thick**
1 **12-ounce jar brown gravy**

● In the same skillet arrange chops. Place potatoes and vegetables over chops. Spoon gravy over all. Cover and cook over medium-low heat for 7 to 8 minutes or till heated through. Serves 4.

You're only four ingredients and 20 minutes away from this hearty one-dish meal.

Beef and Eggplant

Total Time: 25 minutes

1 **pound ground beef *or* lamb**	● In a large skillet cook ground beef or lamb and onion till meat is brown. Drain excess fat from skillet.
1 **medium onion, chopped (½ cup)**	

1 **8-ounce can tomato sauce**	● Stir in tomato sauce, water, oregano, and chili powder. Bring to boiling. Reduce heat. Arrange eggplant slices on top. Cover and simmer for 8 to 10 minutes or till eggplant is tender.
½ **cup water**	
½ **teaspoon dried oregano, crushed**	
½ **teaspoon chili powder**	
1 **small eggplant, cut into ½-inch slices**	

½ **cup shredded cheddar cheese (2 ounces)**	● Remove from heat. Sprinkle eggplant with cheese. Cover and let stand for 1 to 2 minutes or till cheese melts. Sprinkle with parsley, if desired. Makes 4 servings.
2 **tablespoons snipped parsley (optional)**	

To peel or not to peel? The answer is up to you. This dish goes together faster if you leave the peel on the eggplant.

Beefy Sauerkraut Dinner

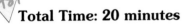

Total Time: 20 minutes

1 **pound ground beef**	● In a large skillet cook ground beef and celery till meat is brown. Drain fat from skillet.
½ **cup sliced celery**	

1 **16-ounce can sauerkraut, rinsed and drained**	● Stir in sauerkraut, tomato sauce, caraway seed, salt, and pepper. Cook till heated through. Remove from heat. Sprinkle with cheese. Cover and let stand for 1 to 2 minutes or till cheese melts. Makes 4 servings.
1 **15-ounce can tomato sauce with tomato tidbits**	
½ **teaspoon caraway seed**	
¼ **teaspoon salt**	
⅛ **teaspoon pepper**	
½ **cup shredded Swiss cheese (2 ounces)**	

Serve this tangy skillet dish with rye bread or rolls for the flavor of a Reuben sandwich.

Total Time: 20 minutes

Creamy Ham And Pasta

6 ounces linguine *or* spaghetti	● Cook the pasta according to the package directions. Drain.
2 medium carrots, sliced 2 tablespoons margarine *or* butter 1 4-ounce can sliced mushrooms, drained 2 tablespoons all-purpose flour ½ teaspoon dried basil, crushed 1 cup milk	● Meanwhile, for sauce, in a 1½-quart microwave-safe casserole combine carrots and margarine. Cover and micro-cook on 100% power (high) for 4 to 5 minutes or till carrots are crisp-tender. Stir in mushrooms, flour, and basil. Add milk. Stir to blend. Cook, uncovered, on high for 3 to 5 minutes or till thickened and bubbly, stirring every minute.
6 ounces sliced fully cooked ham, cut into bite-size strips ½ cup shredded Gruyère cheese (2 ounces)	● Stir in ham strips and cheese. Cover and cook on high for 2 to 3 minutes more or till cheese is melted. Place pasta in serving bowl. Add sauce and toss to coat. Makes 4 servings.

For a spicy dish, substitute prosciutto for the fully cooked ham. Also, reduce the flour to 1 tablespoon if you make this substitution.

Pork Chops Mirepoix

Total Time: 25 minutes

2 pork loin chops, cut ¾ inch thick	● Trim excess fat from chops. Season with salt and pepper. In an 8x8x2-inch microwave-safe baking dish arrange chops with meatiest portions facing the outside of the dish. Cover with vented clear plastic wrap. Micro-cook on 30% power (medium-low) for 9 minutes.
	● Give the dish a half-turn and turn chops over. Cover with vented plastic wrap. Cook on medium-low for 10 to 12 minutes more or till meat is no longer pink. Keep warm.
1 tablespoon margarine *or* butter 1 small onion, finely chopped (⅓ cup) 1 small carrot, finely chopped (⅓ cup) ¼ cup sliced fresh mushrooms ¼ teaspoon dried thyme, crushed ⅛ teaspoon ground red pepper 2 teaspoons dried parsley flakes	● In a 1-quart microwave-safe casserole place margarine or butter. Cook, uncovered, on 100% power (high) for 35 to 40 seconds or till melted. Add onion, carrot, mushrooms, thyme, and red pepper. Cover and cook on high for 3 to 5 minutes or till vegetables are tender, stirring once. Stir in parsley. Spoon vegetable mixture over pork chops. Makes 2 servings.

Red pepper gives a little kick to this French-style dish. Mirepoix (mir PWA) refers to the sautéed vegetables and herbs.

Yogurt-Topped Lamb Chops

Total Time: 15 minutes

4 lamb leg sirloin chops, cut ¾ inch thick	● Trim excess fat from lamb chops. Season with salt and pepper. In an 8x8x2-inch microwave-safe baking dish arrange chops with the meatiest portions facing the outside of the dish. Cover with waxed paper. Micro-cook on 100% power (high) for 3 minutes. Turn chops over. Cook, covered, on high for 2 to 4 minutes more or till desired doneness.
¼ cup plain yogurt 1 tablespoon brown sugar ⅛ teaspoon ground cinnamon Dash onion powder Snipped parsley (optional)	● Meanwhile, for sauce, in a small mixing bowl combine yogurt, brown sugar, cinnamon, and onion powder. Spoon sauce over chops. Sprinkle with parsley, if desired. Makes 4 servings.

An easy, no-cook, cinnamon-charged sauce tops these micro-cooked lamb chops.

Pork Chops Mirepoix

Cajun-Style Meat Ring

Total Time: 25 minutes

1 beaten egg
¾ cup soft bread crumbs
    (1 slice)
¼ cup milk
¼ cup finely chopped onion
½ teaspoon garlic salt
½ teaspoon dried thyme,
    crushed
  Several dashes bottled hot
    pepper sauce
1 pound ground beef

● In a large mixing bowl combine the beaten egg, bread crumbs, milk, onion, garlic salt, thyme, and hot pepper sauce. Add ground beef. Mix well.

To give our meat loaf a Louisiana flavor, we topped it with a peppery tomato sauce and served it with rice.

● In a 9-inch microwave-safe pie plate shape the meat mixture into a 6-inch ring that's 2 inches wide (see photo, below). Cover with waxed paper. Micro-cook on 100% power (high) for 7 to 9 minutes or till no pink remains and meat is done (170°), giving the dish a quarter-turn every 3 minutes. Transfer meat ring to a platter. Cover and keep warm.

1 8-ounce can tomato sauce
¼ cup chopped green pepper
¼ teaspoon celery seed
  Several dashes bottled hot
    pepper sauce
  Hot cooked rice

● For sauce, in a 2-cup microwave-safe measure combine tomato sauce, green pepper, celery seed, and hot pepper sauce. Cover with waxed paper and cook on high for 3 to 4 minutes or till green pepper is tender, stirring once. Spoon some sauce over meat. Serve with rice. Pass remaining sauce. Makes 4 servings.

To shape the meat ring, form the meat mixture into a mound 6 inches in diameter in the pie plate. Push the meat from the center to form a hole about 2 inches in diameter, making a 2-inch-wide meat ring.

Pork with Creamy Bacon Sauce

Total Time: 25 minutes

¾ **pound boneless pork**	● Cut pork on bias into thin bite-size strips. Season with salt and pepper.
1 **tablespoon cooking oil**	● Meanwhile, preheat a 10-inch microwave browning dish on 100% power (high) for 5 minutes. Add the cooking oil. Swirl to coat the dish. Add pork. Micro-cook, covered, on high for 3 to 4 minutes or till the meat is no longer pink, stirring every minute. Use a slotted spoon to remove meat from dish. Set aside.
3 **green onions, cut into 1-inch pieces** 8 **cherry tomatoes, cut into halves** ¼ **cup dairy sour cream** ¼ **cup sour cream and bacon salad dressing** **Grated Parmesan cheese** **Hot cooked spinach** *or* **whole wheat noodles**	● Add onions to the dish. Cook, covered, on high for 1 to 2 minutes or till crisp-tender. Pour off juices. Return meat to dish. Stir in tomatoes, sour cream, and salad dressing. Cook, uncovered, on high for 2 to 3 minutes or till heated through, stirring once. Sprinkle with Parmesan cheese. Serve with noodles. Makes 4 servings.

This easy, creamy sauce starts with bottled sour cream and bacon salad dressing. For a different flavor, use another sour-cream-based dressing.

Sweet-and-Sour Meatballs

Total Time: 25 minutes

1 **beaten egg** ¼ **cup fine dry bread crumbs** 2 **tablespoons snipped parsley** 2 **tablespoons soy sauce** 1 **pound ground beef**	● In a medium mixing bowl combine egg, bread crumbs, parsley, and soy sauce. Add ground beef. Mix well. Shape into 12 meatballs. Place in an 8x8x2-inch microwave-safe baking dish. Cover with waxed paper. Micro-cook on 100% power (high) for 5 to 7 minutes or till no pink remains, rearranging and turning meatballs over once. Remove meatballs; drain on paper towels. Drain fat from dish.
1 **16-ounce can peach slices** 1 **cup sweet-and-sour sauce** 2 **tablespoons sliced green onion** **Hot cooked rice**	● Drain peaches, reserving 2 tablespoons syrup. In the same dish, combine peaches, the reserved peach syrup, sweet-and-sour sauce, and onion. Cook, uncovered, on high for 3 to 4 minutes or till heated through, stirring once. Stir in meatballs. Cook, uncovered, on high for 1 to 2 minutes more or till heated through. Serve with hot cooked rice. Makes 4 servings.

For fast-fix dishes, choose quick-cooking rice. It cooks in less than half the time of regular rice.

**Beef Paprikash
With Potatoes**

Beef Paprikash With Potatoes

Total Time: 25 minutes

4 large baking potatoes	● Scrub potatoes. Prick skins with a fork. Arrange in a spoke pattern on a microwave-safe plate or paper towel in microwave oven, leaving 1 inch of space between potatoes. Micro-cook, uncovered, on 100% power (high) for 16 to 20 minutes or till potatoes are tender, rearranging once.
1 pound ground beef 1 12-ounce jar brown gravy 1 cup frozen peas 1 8-ounce container sour cream dip with toasted onion 1 tablespoon paprika ⅛ teaspoon garlic powder ⅛ teaspoon pepper	● Meanwhile, in a large skillet, cook beef till brown. Drain fat from skillet. Stir in gravy, peas, *half* of the sour cream dip, paprika, garlic powder, and pepper. Cook for 3 to 4 minutes or till peas are crisp-tender.
	● To serve, cut potatoes lengthwise into quarters and arrange on individual serving plates. Spoon the beef mixture over potatoes. Top with remaining sour cream dip. Makes 4 servings.

To make the best use of time, we cooked the meat mixture conventionally and micro-cooked the potatoes.

Easy Veal Cordon Bleu

SUPER FAST

Total Time: 15 minutes

4 veal cubed steaks (about 1 pound total)	● Place veal in a 12x7½x2-inch microwave-safe baking dish. Sprinkle with salt and pepper. Cover with waxed paper. Micro-cook on 100% power (high) for 3 minutes. Turn veal over and rearrange in dish. Cook, covered, on high for 2 to 4 minutes more or till meat is no longer pink. Drain off fat.
4 slices Swiss cheese (4 ounces) 4 thin slices fully cooked ham (about 3 ounces) Paprika	● Cut the cheese slices in half. Place half of a cheese slice on each veal steak. Top each with a ham slice and then, the remaining half of cheese slice. Cook, uncovered, on high for 1 to 2 minutes or till the cheese is melted. Sprinkle with paprika. Makes 4 servings.

In the traditional recipe for Veal Cordon Bleu, the veal wraps around the ham and cheese. We simplified this recipe by just placing the ham and cheese over the veal.

Total Time: 15 minutes

Saucy Swiss Veal

1 tablespoon cooking oil
4 veal cubed steaks

● Preheat a 10-inch microwave browning dish on 100% power (high) for 5 minutes. Add cooking oil. Swirl to coat dish. Season veal with salt and pepper. Add veal to browning dish.
  Micro-cook, uncovered, on high for 3 to 4 minutes or till no pink remains, turning veal over after 2 minutes. Transfer to serving platter. Keep warm.

To ensure a smooth cheese sauce every time, we used process cheese.

½ cup milk
2 teaspoons all-purpose flour
1 2½-ounce can sliced mushrooms, drained
½ cup shredded process Swiss cheese (2 ounces)
1 tablespoon dried snipped chives

● For sauce, in a 2-cup microwave-safe measure combine milk and flour. Stir in mushrooms. Cook, uncovered, on high for 1 minute. Stir sauce. Cook for 1 to 2 minutes more or till sauce is thickened and bubbly, stirring every 30 seconds.
  Stir in Swiss cheese and chives. Cook 30 to 60 seconds more or till cheese is melted. Spoon cheese sauce over veal steaks. Makes 4 servings.

Ham with Cucumber Sauce

Total Time: 10 minutes

1 1½- to 2-pound fully cooked ham slice

● Place ham in a 10x6x2-inch microwave-safe baking dish. Cover with waxed paper. Micro-cook on 100% power (high) for 8 to 10 minutes or till heated through, turning ham over after 5 minutes.

Pictured on pages 4 and 5.

How do you cook a main dish in just 10 minutes and keep your cool, too? Try this ham slice with a refreshing cucumber and dill sauce.

½ of a medium cucumber
1 8-ounce carton plain yogurt *or* dairy sour cream
1 tablespoon milk
1 teaspoon dried snipped chives
¼ teaspoon dried dillweed

● Meanwhile, chop the cucumber. In a small mixing bowl stir together cucumber, yogurt or sour cream, milk, chives, and dillweed. Serve cucumber mixture over ham. Makes 6 servings.

Chili-Stuffed Peppers

SUPER FAST

Total Time: 15 minutes

1 15½-ounce can chili with beans ½ cup quick-cooking rice ¼ cup red salsa 2 teaspoons Worcestershire sauce	● In a 1½-quart microwave-safe casserole combine chili, rice, salsa, and Worcestershire sauce. Micro-cook, covered, on 100% power (high) for 3 to 5 minutes or till bubbly. Stir chili mixture. Cover and set aside.
2 medium green peppers 2 tablespoons water	● Meanwhile, cut green peppers in half lengthwise and remove seeds. Place pepper halves, cut side down, in an 8x8x2-inch microwave-safe baking dish. Add water. Cover with vented clear plastic wrap. Cook on high for 3 to 5 minutes or till the peppers are crisp-tender, giving dish a half-turn once. Drain the peppers, cut side down, on paper towels.
½ cup shredded Monterey Jack cheese with jalapeño peppers, (2 ounces)	● Arrange the pepper halves, cut side up, in the 8x8x2-inch baking dish. Spoon the chili mixture into the pepper halves. Cover with waxed paper. Cook on high for 2 to 3 minutes or till chili mixture is heated through, giving the dish a half-turn once. Sprinkle with cheese. Cook, uncovered, on high about 30 seconds or till cheese is melted. Makes 2 servings.

For those of you who like fiery foods, use the hot-style chili. If you prefer less spicy foods, use plain Monterey Jack cheese.

Attention, Microwave Owners

Recipes with microwave directions were tested in countertop microwave ovens that operate on 600 to 700 watts. Cooking times are approximate since microwave ovens vary by manufacturer.

Meatball Drop Soup

Total Time: 35 minutes

| 1 | 16- *or* 20-ounce package frozen vegetables for stew |
| 1 | cup water |

● In a 3-quart saucepan combine frozen vegetables and water. Bring mixture to boiling. Reduce heat. Cover and simmer for 10 minutes.

Shaping meatballs is a cinch in this hearty soup. Just spoon the herb-flavored meat mixture into the simmering broth.

1	beaten egg
¼	cup fine dry bread crumbs
¼	cup milk
½	teaspoon salt
¼	teaspoon dried marjoram, crushed
1	pound lean ground beef

● Meanwhile, in a medium mixing bowl combine egg, bread crumbs, milk, salt, and marjoram. Add ground beef. Mix well. Set aside.

| 1 | 15-ounce can herb tomato sauce |
| 1 | 12-ounce jar brown gravy |

● Stir tomato sauce and gravy into vegetable mixture. Bring to boiling. Reduce heat. Drop beef mixture by small spoonfuls into the simmering mixture. Cover and cook for 10 to 12 minutes or till the meatballs are no longer pink and the vegetables are tender, stirring occasionally. Makes 5 servings.

Beer and Bean Chili

Total Time: 35 minutes

1 pound ground beef *or* pork
1 large onion, chopped (1 cup)
1 medium carrot, shredded (½ cup)
½ cup chopped green pepper

● In a Dutch oven cook ground beef or pork, onion, carrot, and green pepper till the meat is brown. Drain off fat.

2 15-ounce cans great northern beans
1 16-ounce can tomatoes, cut up
1 12-ounce can beer
1 6-ounce can tomato paste
2 tablespoons chili powder
½ teaspoon garlic salt

● Stir in *undrained* beans, *undrained* tomatoes, beer, tomato paste, chili powder, and garlic salt. Bring to boiling. Reduce heat. Cover and simmer for 15 to 20 minutes or till flavors are blended, stirring occasionally. Serves 5 or 6.

If you have any chili left over, freeze the extra. Reheat the chili in a saucepan. Or, if you have a microwave oven, heat, covered, on 70 percent power (medium-high), allowing 5 to 6 minutes per cup of chili.

SUPER FAST

Quick Beef Noodle Soup

Total Time: 20 minutes

¾ pound beef top round steak
1 tablespoon cooking oil

● Cut the round steak into thin, bite-size strips. In a large saucepan heat the oil over medium-high heat. Add the beef. Cook and stir for 3 to 4 minutes or till the beef is brown. Remove beef and set aside. Drain off fat.

1 3-ounce package Oriental noodles with beef flavor
4 cups beef broth
1½ cups loose-pack frozen mixed vegetables
1 cup water
1 stalk celery, thinly sliced
2 tablespoons soy sauce

● Break up the noodles. In the same saucepan combine noodles, seasoning packet, beef broth, mixed vegetables, water, celery, and soy sauce. Bring to boiling. Reduce heat. Cover and simmer about 5 minutes or till vegetables and noodles are tender. Stir in beef. Heat through. Makes 4 servings.

After adding the steak to the soup, cook the soup just enough to warm up the steak. Don't overcook or the meat will be tough.

Hamburger Minestrone

Total Time: 25 minutes

¾ **pound ground beef** 1 **medium onion, chopped** **(½ cup)**	● In a large saucepan cook beef and onion over medium-high heat till meat is brown and onion is tender. Drain off fat.
1½ **cups loose-pack frozen** **zucchini, carrots,** **cauliflower, lima beans,** **and Italian beans** 1 **16-ounce can tomatoes,** **cut up** 1 **8-ounce can red kidney** **beans** 1 **cup beef broth** ½ **cup dry red wine** 1 **teaspoon bottled minced** **garlic** *or* ¼ **teaspoon** **garlic powder** 1 **teaspoon Italian** **seasoning**	● Stir in frozen vegetables, *undrained* tomatoes, *undrained* kidney beans, beef broth, wine, garlic, and Italian seasoning. Bring to boiling.
⅓ **cup tiny shell macaroni** *or* **other small pasta** **Grated Parmesan cheese**	● Stir in macaroni. Reduce heat. Cover and simmer for 8 to 10 minutes or till macaroni and vegetables are tender. Season with salt and pepper. To serve, ladle into soup bowls and sprinkle with cheese. Makes 4 servings.

Our timesaving version of this popular vegetable soup uses ground beef and frozen mixed vegetables.

Shortcut Irish Stew

Total Time: 25 minutes

1 **pound ground lamb** 1 **medium onion, chopped** **(½ cup)**	● In a large saucepan cook the lamb and onion over medium-high heat till meat is brown. Drain off fat.
2 **12-ounce jars brown gravy** 1 **medium potato, peeled** **and chopped (1 cup)** 1 **medium turnip, peeled** **and chopped (1 cup)** 1 **teaspoon dried savory,** **crushed** 1 **cup frozen peas**	● Stir in gravy, potato, turnip, and savory. Bring to boiling. Reduce heat. Cover and simmer about 12 minutes or till the vegetables are almost tender. Stir in frozen peas. Cover and cook for 3 to 5 minutes more or till peas are crisp-tender. Makes 4 servings.

We streamlined Irish stew by substituting ground lamb for meat cubes and using prepared gravy for the broth.

Easy Swiss Ham Chowder

Total Time: 20 minutes

1½ cups cubed fully cooked ham
1½ cups shredded cabbage
1 17-ounce can cream-style corn
1 cup chicken broth
1 cup milk
⅛ teaspoon pepper

● In a large saucepan combine ham, cabbage, *undrained* corn, chicken broth, milk, and pepper. Bring to boiling. Reduce heat. Cover and simmer about 5 minutes or till cabbage is crisp-tender.

Always a favorite combo, ham and Swiss cheese team up in this cabbage and corn soup.

2 slices (2 ounces) process Swiss cheese
2 tablespoons snipped parsley

● Tear cheese into pieces. Add to saucepan, stirring till melted. To serve, ladle into soup bowls. Sprinkle parsley over each serving. Makes 4 servings.

Ham and Squash Soup

Total Time: 20 minutes

1 12-ounce package frozen mashed cooked winter squash
1 10-ounce package frozen lima beans
1 cup chicken broth
1 medium onion, chopped (½ cup)
¼ teaspoon ground nutmeg
⅛ teaspoon pepper

● In a large saucepan combine squash, lima beans, chicken broth, onion, nutmeg, and pepper. Bring to boiling. Reduce heat. Cover and simmer about 10 minutes or till lima beans and onion are tender and squash is thawed.

What could be easier? Just simmer the vegetables in chicken broth and stir in the ham and milk. Then ring the dinner bell. Soup's on.

2 cups cubed fully cooked ham
1 5-ounce can (⅔ cup) evaporated milk

● Stir in ham and milk. Cook, covered, for 2 to 3 minutes or till mixture is heated through. Makes 4 servings.

Bratwurst-Cheese Soup

Total Time: 25 minutes

¼ **cup margarine** *or* **butter**
2 **carrots, shredded**
1 **stalk celery, thinly sliced**

● In a large saucepan melt the margarine or butter. Add carrots and celery. Cook till tender.

¼ **cup all-purpose flour**
⅛ **teaspoon pepper**
4 **cups milk**
8 **ounces smoked bratwurst, sliced**

● Stir in flour and pepper till blended. Add milk and bratwurst. Cook and stir over medium heat about 8 minutes or till mixture is thickened and bubbly. Cook and stir for 1 minute more.

2 **cups shredded American** *or* **process Swiss cheese (8 ounces)**

● Add cheese. Cook, stirring constantly, till cheese is melted. Makes 4 servings.

Beef Vinaigrette Salad

SUPER FAST

Total Time: 15 minutes

¾ **pound beef top round steak**
3 **tablespoons cooking oil**
2 **tablespoons lemon juice**
½ **teaspoon salt**
½ **teaspoon Italian seasoning**
⅛ **teaspoon pepper**
1 **tablespoon cooking oil**

● Cut steak on bias into thin bite-size strips. For dressing, in a screw-top jar combine oil, lemon juice, salt, Italian seasoning, and pepper. Cover and shake well. Set aside.

Preheat a wok or large skillet over high heat. Add cooking oil. Stir-fry beef in hot oil for 2 to 3 minutes or till brown. Drain fat from wok.

1 **cup sliced fresh mushrooms**
1 **small zucchini, sliced**
8 **cherry tomatoes, cut in halves**
Lettuce leaves

● Add vegetables and dressing to wok or skillet. Cook and stir for 1 to 2 minutes or till zucchini is crisp-tender. To serve, arrange beef mixture and vegetables on lettuce leaves. Serves 3.

To make the most efficient use of your time, cut up the beef and vegetables before you begin to stir-fry.

Beef and Pasta Salad

Total Time: 45 minutes

4 **ounces corkscrew macaroni**
1 **10-ounce package frozen cut broccoli**

● Cook pasta in a large amount of boiling salted water for 9 minutes. Add broccoli. Return to boiling. Cook for 2 to 3 minutes more or till broccoli is crisp-tender. Drain in colander. Rinse with cold water. Drain again.

6 **ounces thinly sliced cooked beef**
1 **6-ounce jar marinated artichoke hearts, drained**
2 **small tomatoes, cut into small wedges**
1 **cup crumbled feta cheese (4 ounces)**

● Meanwhile, cut the beef into julienne strips. Cut up any large artichokes. In a large serving bowl combine beef, artichoke hearts, tomatoes, feta cheese, and pasta mixture.

½ **cup Caesar salad dressing**

● Add dressing to salad. Toss to coat. Place in the freezer for 10 to 15 minutes to chill, if desired. Makes 4 servings.

If you prefer peeled tomatoes in your salad, just dip the tomatoes into the boiling water before you cook the pasta. The skins will slip right off.

Ham and Bulgur Salad

Total Time: 25 minutes

1 11-ounce can mandarin orange sections *or* pineapple tidbits and mandarin orange sections
2 cups water
1 cup bulgur wheat

● Place oranges in the freezer to chill. Meanwhile, in a medium saucepan combine water and bulgur. Bring to boiling. Remove from heat. Cover and let stand 15 minutes or till tender.

To avoid quick-chilling the oranges in the freezer, place the can of oranges in the refrigerator the night before so they'll be cold when you're ready to add them to the salad.

⅓ cup mayonnaise *or* salad dressing
⅓ cup plain yogurt
1 teaspoon Dijon-style mustard
⅛ teaspoon pepper
2 cups cut-up fully cooked ham
1 stalk celery, sliced
2 green onions, sliced

● Meanwhile, in a large serving bowl stir together mayonnaise or salad dressing, yogurt, mustard, and pepper. Stir in ham, celery, and green onion. Drain bulgur. Rinse with cold water. Drain again.

Add to mixture in bowl. Toss to coat. Drain oranges and fold into salad. Place salad in freezer for 5 to 10 minutes to chill, if desired. Makes 4 servings.

Greens Make the Salad

Dress up any salad with a bed of fresh greens. Leaf lettuce, iceberg lettuce, and romaine all make good liners as whole leaves or torn into bite-size pieces. For another time, shred some cabbage or iceberg lettuce. Or, use cabbage or butterhead lettuce leaves as serving cups for salad.

Chili-Be

Chili-Beef Salad

Total Time: 20 minutes

1 pound ground beef *or* bulk pork sausage
1 medium onion, chopped (½ cup)
1 7½-ounce can tomatoes, cut up
¼ cup catsup
1 tablespoon chili powder

● In a large skillet cook beef or sausage and onion till meat is brown. Drain fat from skillet. Stir in *undrained* tomatoes, catsup, and chili powder. Bring to boiling. Reduce heat and simmer, uncovered, for 8 to 10 minutes or till desired consistency.

4 cups shredded lettuce
1 cup shredded cheddar cheese (4 ounces)
8 pitted ripe olives, sliced
½ of an 8-ounce carton dairy sour cream
Snipped cilantro *or* parsley
Tortilla chips (optional)

● Arrange lettuce on each of 4 plates. Spoon meat mixture over lettuce. Sprinkle each with cheese and olives. Top with sour cream and cilantro or parsley. Serve with tortilla chips, if desired. Makes 4 servings.

Cool the spicy flavor of this taco-style salad with lots of sour cream. If you like a thinner dressing, stir a little milk into the sour cream.

Ham and Salami Slaw

Total Time: 30 minutes

½ of a 16-ounce package (4 cups) coleslaw mix
1 small zucchini, sliced
1 small onion, chopped

● In a large serving bowl combine coleslaw mix, zucchini, and onion.

4 ounces thinly sliced fully cooked ham
4 ounces thinly sliced salami
1 4-ounce package (1 cup) shredded mozzarella *or* cheddar cheese

● Cut ham and salami into thin bite-size strips. Add ham, salami, and cheese to cabbage mixture. Toss lightly to mix.

½ cup creamy Italian salad dressing

● Pour dressing over salad. Toss lightly to coat. Makes 4 servings.

Check out the produce aisle for a mixture of shredded cabbage and other vegetables packaged as a coleslaw mix. Or, make your own. Combine 3 cups shredded cabbage and 1 cup shredded carrot or other vegetables.

Curried Pork Salad

Total Time: 15 minutes

8 ounces cooked pork *or* lamb	● Trim excess fat from meat. Cut the pork or lamb into bite-size pieces. Place the meat in a large serving bowl.
2 cups chilled cooked rice 1 8-ounce can sliced water chestnuts, drained 1 8-ounce can pineapple tidbits, drained ½ cup chopped cashews *or* peanuts ¼ cup chopped green pepper	● Add chilled rice, water chestnuts, pineapple tidbits, nuts, and green pepper to meat. Mix well.
½ cup dairy sour cream ½ cup mayonnaise *or* salad dressing 1 tablespoon lemon juice 1 teaspoon curry powder	● In a small mixing bowl stir together sour cream, mayonnaise or salad dressing, lemon juice, and curry powder. Add to meat mixture. Toss to coat. Makes 4 servings.

For the coldest, fastest rice, prepare quick-cooking rice according to package directions. Rinse with cold water and chill in the freezer about 15 minutes.

Ham and Cottage Cheese Salad

Total Time: 15 minutes

1 cup cream-style cottage cheese ⅓ cup creamy Italian salad dressing 1 small carrot, shredded 2 tablespoons sliced green onion	● Stir together cottage cheese, salad dressing, carrot, and green onion.
1 16-ounce can sliced potatoes, drained 1 8-ounce package sliced chopped ham, cut into strips Lettuce leaves	● Arrange potatoes and ham on each of 4 lettuce-lined plates. Top with cottage cheese mixture. Makes 4 servings.

Be prepared. Store canned foods you plan to use for salads in the refrigerator. That way, they'll be ice-cold when you're ready to make the salad.

Ham and Avocado Salad

Total Time: 30 minutes

4 cups torn romaine *or* leaf lettuce **2 green onions, sliced** **1 medium carrot, shredded** **1 medium avocado** **Lemon juice**	● Line 3 plates with romaine or lettuce. Sprinkle with green onions and carrot. Cut the avocado in half. Remove seed and peel. Slice avocado lengthwise. Brush with lemon juice. Arrange avocado slices on salad plates.
6 ounces thinly sliced fully cooked ham **2 ounces Muenster, mozzarella, *or* provolone cheese, cut into cubes**	● Fold each ham slice in thirds. Arrange ham and cheese on salad plates.
6 tablespoons spices and herbs salad dressing *or* other clear salad dressing	● Sprinkle 2 tablespoons salad dressing over each salad. Makes 3 servings.

Here's a Test Kitchen tip for fast-fixin' salads: Use romaine for salad greens. Its long, firm leaves are quicker to clean than those of other greens.

Easy Fajitas

Total Time: 25 minutes

1	6-ounce container frozen avocado dip (optional)

● Thaw frozen avocado dip overnight in the refrigerator, if desired.

8	8-inch flour tortillas
1	pound ground beef
1	medium green pepper, cut into thin strips
1	small onion, thinly sliced
½	of a 0.7-ounce package dry Italian salad dressing mix

● Wrap flour tortillas in foil. Warm in a 350° oven for 10 minutes.
   Meanwhile, in a large skillet cook ground beef, green pepper, and onion about 5 minutes or till meat is brown and vegetables are tender. Remove from heat. Drain fat from skillet. Stir salad dressing mix into the meat mixture.

Red *or* green salsa
Dairy sour cream
Shredded cheddar cheese
Lettuce leaves *or* other greens

● Arrange the beef mixture down the center of tortillas. Top with avocado dip, salsa, sour cream, and cheese. Roll tortillas around filling. Serve on lettuce-lined plates and top with additional dip, salsa, and cheese. Makes 4 servings.

To speed up this recipe, soften the tortillas in the microwave. Wrap them in plastic wrap. Micro-cook on 100% power (high) for 35 to 40 seconds or till they're soft.

Bratwurst and Sauerkraut Rolls

Total Time: 40 minutes

8 smoked bratwurst (about
   1½ pounds total)
2 tablespoons Dijon-style
   mustard
2 slices Swiss cheese
½ of an 8-ounce can
   sauerkraut, rinsed and
   drained

● Slit each bratwurst lengthwise, cutting just to but not through the opposite side. Spread the cut surfaces with mustard. Cut each cheese slice into 4 strips. Insert one cheese strip and some sauerkraut into each bratwurst.

Can a round peg fit into a triangle? This sandwich is as close as you'll get— bratwurst links wrapped in crescent dough triangles.

1 package (8) refrigerated
   crescent rolls
   Caraway seed

● Separate crescent rolls into triangles. Wrap a triangle of dough around each bratwurst. Place, seam side up, on a baking sheet. Moisten dough with water. Sprinkle with caraway seed. Bake in a 375° oven about 18 minutes or till golden. Makes 8 servings.

Frankfurter Barbecue Curls

Total Time: 20 minutes

6 frankfurters

● Preheat the broiler. Cut crosswise slashes in each frankfurter at ½-inch intervals, cutting to but not through the other side (see photo, right).

1 8-ounce can tomato sauce
¼ cup apricot *or* pineapple
   preserves
1 teaspoon Worcestershire
   sauce
1 teaspoon dried minced
   onion

● In a medium skillet combine tomato sauce, preserves, Worcestershire sauce, and onion. Add the frankfurters. Bring to boiling. Reduce heat. Cover and simmer about 5 minutes or till frankfurters curl and are heated through.

Slashing the frankfurters makes them curl as they cook, so they nestle right into the hamburger buns. It's easy to do. Take a sharp knife and cut almost, but not quite, through the frankfurter. Continue making cuts every ½ inch.

6 slices American *or*
   Swiss cheese
6 hamburger buns, split

● Meanwhile, place a slice of cheese on the bottom half of each bun. Place both halves of buns on a baking sheet. Broil 4 to 5 inches from heat for 1 to 2 minutes or till cheese begins to melt and buns are toasted. Place a frankfurter on the bottom half of each bun. Spoon some sauce over each and top with bun top. Makes 6 servings.

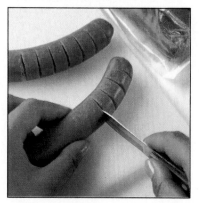

Cheese-Stuffed Burgers

Total Time: 25 minutes

1 beaten egg
¼ cup fine dry bread crumbs
3 tablespoons buttermilk salad dressing
1 pound ground beef
2 ounces Monterey Jack, cheddar, *or* Swiss cheese

● Preheat the broiler. Meanwhile, in a medium mixing bowl combine egg, bread crumbs, and salad dressing. Add ground beef. Mix well. Shape meat mixture into eight ¼-inch-thick patties.

Cut the cheese into 4 pieces. Place cheese on *four* of the patties. Top with remaining patties. Press meat around edges to seal.

● Place patties on the unheated rack of a broiler pan. Broil 3 to 4 inches from heat for 6 minutes. Turn patties over. Broil for 6 to 8 minutes more or till meat is no longer pink.

4 lettuce leaves
4 hamburger buns, split and toasted
4 tomato slices
Buttermilk salad dressing (optional)

● Serve burgers on lettuce-lined buns with tomato slices and additional salad dressing, if desired. Makes 4 servings.

Pocket these burgers in pita bread. Choose large whole wheat or plain rounds, and cut them in half crosswise. Serve one burger in each half.

Cheese-Beef Croissant
Sandwiches

Cheese-Beef Croissant Sandwiches

SUPER FAST

Total Time: 15 minutes

¼ cup mayonnaise *or* salad dressing 2 teaspoons horseradish mustard 1 teaspoon poppy seed ¼ teaspoon onion powder	● For dressing, stir together mayonnaise or salad dressing, mustard, poppy seed, and onion powder. Set aside.
4 croissants	● Split the croissants in half lengthwise. Spread the bottom half of each croissant with dressing.
4 lettuce leaves 8 ounces thinly sliced cooked beef 2 slices cheddar, Swiss, *or* Monterey Jack cheese, cut in half (3 ounces) ½ cup alfalfa sprouts	● Top each croissant bottom with lettuce, beef, cheese, and alfalfa sprouts. Top with croissant top. Serve with remaining dressing. Makes 4 servings.

Use the poppy seed dressing on other meat sandwiches, too.

Ham and Apple Sandwiches

SUPER FAST

Total Time: 10 minutes

1 3-ounce package very thinly sliced ham ½ of an 8-ounce container (½ cup) soft-style cream cheese ½ cup shredded cheddar cheese 1 small apple, chopped ⅛ teaspoon ground cinnamon	● Coarsely chop the ham. In a small mixing bowl stir together ham, cream cheese, cheddar cheese, chopped apple, and cinnamon.
6 slices whole wheat bread, toasted	● Spread half of the bread slices with the ham mixture. Top with remaining bread slices. Makes 3 servings.

This sandwich makes it easier for you to get your apple a day. We packed one into the ham and cheese spread.

Open-Face Bacon Sandwiches

SUPER FAST

Total Time: 15 minutes

¼ cup maple *or* maple-flavored syrup 1 teaspoon prepared mustard	● In a small saucepan combine syrup and mustard. Cook till heated through. Keep warm.
1 tablespoon margarine *or* butter 8 thin slices Canadian-style bacon	● In a large skillet melt the margarine or butter. Add bacon and cook till light brown on both sides.
2 English muffins, split and toasted 1 8¼-ounce can pineapple slices, drained	● Place *2* bacon slices on *each* English muffin half. Top *each* with a pineapple slice. Serve with syrup. Makes 2 servings.

The next time you're hankering for a hearty breakfast try this pineapple-topped sandwich.

Sausage And Pepper Sandwiches

Total Time: 30 minutes

1 pound Italian sausage links 1 small onion, thinly sliced ½ cup water 1 large green pepper, cut into 1-inch pieces	● In a large skillet combine sausage, onion, and water. Bring to boiling. Reduce heat. Simmer, covered, 10 minutes. Add green pepper. Simmer, covered, 3 to 5 minutes or till sausage is brown. Drain liquid from skillet.
1 8-ounce can pizza sauce	● Add pizza sauce to sausage and vegetables. Cook till heated through.
4 hoagie buns, split and toasted Grated Parmesan cheese	● Spoon sausage, onion, and pepper into buns. Top with sauce. Sprinkle with Parmesan cheese. Makes 4 servings.

Tackle these sandwiches with a knife and fork for easier going.

Colossal Corned Beef On Rye

SUPER FAST

Total Time: 20 minutes

1	**1-pound round loaf unsliced pumpernickel *or* rye bread** **Dijon-style *or* horseradish mustard**

● Cut a 2-inch-thick slice off the top of the loaf. Using a fork, hollow out the loaf, leaving a shell about ½ inch thick. Spread the cut side of the top slice with mustard. Set aside.

8	**ounces thinly sliced corned beef**
1	**cup shredded Swiss cheese (4 ounces)**
½	**cup creamy cole slaw**
1	**medium tomato, chopped**

● To assemble the sandwich, arrange *one-third* of the corned beef in the bottom of the shell. Top with *half* of the Swiss cheese, *half* of the cole slaw, and *half* of the tomato. Repeat the layers. Add remaining corned beef. Top with the bread slice. To serve, cut into wedges. Makes 6 servings.

To make the bread shell for this jumbo sandwich, cut a slice off the top of the loaf, about a third of the way down. Using a fork, gently remove the bread from inside the loaf, leaving behind a ½-inch-thick shell.

Greek Lamb Pitas

Total Time: 30 minutes

¾ **pound boneless lamb *or*
    beef top round steak**
½ **cup plain yogurt**
1 **tablespoon all-purpose
    flour**
¾ **teaspoon Italian
    seasoning**
¼ **teaspoon garlic powder**

● Cut lamb or beef on the bias into thin bite-size strips. Stir together yogurt, flour, Italian seasoning, and garlic powder.

Turn this Mediterranean stir-fry into a main-dish salad by spooning the lamb filling over spinach or other greens.

1 **tablespoon cooking oil**
1 **medium onion, chopped**
½ **of a small cucumber,
    sliced**

● Preheat a wok or large skillet over high heat. Add oil. (Add more oil as necessary during cooking.) Add the lamb and onion. Stir-fry about 3 minutes or till lamb loses its pink color. Stir in yogurt mixture. Reduce heat. Cook and stir till sauce is thickened and bubbly. Cook and stir for 1 minute more. Remove from heat. Stir in cucumber.

2 **large pita bread rounds,
    halved crosswise**

● Spoon lamb mixture into pita halves. Makes 4 servings.

Total Time: 20 minutes

Oriental Pork Sandwiches

¾ pound pork tenderloin, cut crosswise into 4 pieces 1 tablespoon cooking oil	● Place each piece of pork between 2 sheets of clear plastic wrap. Lightly pound with the flat side of a meat mallet to ¼- to ⅛-inch thickness. Heat a large skillet over medium-high heat. Add the oil. Cook the pork for 4 minutes. Turn pork and cook 2 to 4 minutes more or till no longer pink. Remove the pork from the skillet.
2 tablespoons sliced green onion 2 teaspoons sesame seed 2 tablespoons water 2 tablespoons dry sherry 2 tablespoons teriyaki sauce	● For sauce, add green onion and sesame seed to drippings in the skillet. Cook, stirring constantly, about 1 minute or till sesame seed is toasted. Stir in water, sherry, and teriyaki sauce. Cook till heated through. Remove from heat.
4 kaiser rolls, split and toasted Lettuce leaves *or* shredded cabbage	● To assemble sandwiches, top each roll bottom with lettuce or cabbage and pork. Drizzle some of the sauce over pork. Top with roll tops. Makes 4 servings.

This sandwich is American, but the flavor is Oriental. For even more Oriental flavor, use bok choy or Chinese cabbage in place of the lettuce or cabbage.

Hot Sandwiches To Go

When you're on the run, choose one of these enticing sandwiches. They're quick to make and quick to eat.

● *Ham and Veggie Roll:* Cut a thin slice off the top of a *round club roll.* Hollow out the bottom, leaving a ½-inch shell. Pile very thin slices of *cooked ham* inside the roll bottom. Fill the roll with a drained *marinated vegetable salad* from the deli. Top with *havarti cheese slices.* Broil a minute or two to melt the cheese. Recap with the roll top.

● *Beef and Slaw Barbecue Bun:* Toss bite-size strips of *cooked beef* with *barbecue sauce* mixed with a little *prepared horseradish.* Heat in a saucepan. Pile meat mixture onto the bottom of a split *hoagie roll.* Top with *coleslaw* and roll top.

● *Meat-Loaf Burrito:* Brush a *tortilla* with water to soften. Top with a *lettuce leaf* and *dairy sour cream.* Stack on *cooked meat loaf* and *cheddar cheese slices,* *avocado wedges,* and *onion slices.* Add *sweet pepper pieces* and *salsa.* Roll up. Fasten with a wooden toothpick. Heat in a microwave oven on 100% power (high) for ½ to 1 minute.

Beef Steak Wellington

Total Time: 45 minutes

½	of a 17¼-ounce package (1 sheet) frozen puff pastry sheets
1	tablespoon cooking oil
4	beef tenderloin steaks, cut 1 inch thick (about 1 pound total)

● Remove pastry sheet from freezer. Let stand at room temperature for 20 minutes. Meanwhile, in a 12-inch skillet heat cooking oil. Add steaks and brown over medium-high heat for 1 minute on each side. Remove from heat. Set aside.

A minute saved is a minute earned. To reduce your preparation time, let the puff pastry thaw overnight in the refrigerator.

1	4-ounce can mushroom stems and pieces, drained
1	tablespoon snipped parsley
¼	teaspoon garlic salt
	Dash pepper

● In a small bowl combine mushrooms, parsley, garlic salt, and pepper. Set aside.
  Unfold the puff pastry sheet and place on a lightly floured surface. Cut into 4 rectangles. Roll each piece into a 6-inch square. Place ¼ of the mushroom mixture in the center of each square. Place a steak on top. Moisten edges of pastry with water. Fold pastry over meat. Pinch edges to seal. Place seam-side down in a shallow baking pan.

	Milk
¼	cup whipping cream
1	teaspoon prepared horseradish

● Brush pastry with milk. Bake in a 450° oven for 12 to 14 minutes or till pastry is brown.
  Meanwhile, combine whipping cream and horseradish. Beat with a rotary beater till soft peaks form. Serve with steaks. Makes 4 servings.

Shortcut Favorites

▲▲▲▲▲▲▲▲▲▲▲▲▲▲▲▲▲▲▲▲▲▲▲▲▲▲▲

On the following pages, you'll find recipes for traditional dishes adapted to the way people cook today. We started with classic recipes and streamlined them by substituting ingredients and omitting unnecessary steps. The results taste as good as ever!

Prosciutto-Stuffed Beef

SUPER FAST
Total Time: 20 minutes

1 ounce sliced prosciutto, chopped **1 small carrot, shredded** **1 green onion, sliced**	● Preheat the broiler. For stuffing, combine prosciutto, carrot, and green onion. Set aside.
4 beef tenderloin steaks, cut 1 inch thick **4 thin slices prosciutto**	● Cut a slit horizontally in each steak to form a pocket. Fill pockets with stuffing. Cut prosciutto into 1-inch-wide strips. Wrap the prosciutto around each steak. Secure with wooden toothpicks.
	● Place steaks on the unheated rack of a broiler pan. Broil 3 to 4 inches from the heat for 6 minutes. Turn steaks. Broil to desired doneness (allow 6 to 8 minutes for medium). Makes 4 servings.

Beef tenderloin steak, the tenderest of all steaks, goes by many names. Look for it labeled as filet mignon, beef fillet steak, *filet de boeuf,* and beef tender steak.

SUPER FAST

Total Time: 20 minutes

Veal Piccata

1 **pound veal leg round steak *or* sirloin steak, cut ¼ inch thick** **Lemon pepper**	● Sprinkle veal lightly with salt and lemon pepper. In a large skillet melt margarine or butter. (Add more margarine, as necessary, during cooking.) Cook veal, 2 or 3 pieces at a time, in margarine for 1 to 2 minutes on each side or till brown. Transfer veal to a serving platter. Keep warm.
2 **tablespoons margarine *or* butter**	

1 **tablespoon lemon juice**	● For sauce, add lemon juice and water to the skillet. Cook and stir over low heat till warm, scraping up crusty brown bits from the pan. Stir in parsley. Spoon sauce over veal. Garnish with lemon slices, if desired. Makes 4 servings.
1 **tablespoon water**	
1 **tablespoon snipped parsley**	
1 **lemon, thinly sliced (optional)**	

Look for thinly sliced veal steak, sometimes labeled scallopini or cutlet. If you can't find it, buy ½-inch-thick round steak and pound it to ¼-inch thickness.

Pork with Cider And Cream

Total Time: 25 minutes

¾ **pound pork tenderloin**	● Cut the pork tenderloin into 1-inch-thick slices. Place each piece of pork between 2 sheets of clear plastic wrap. Lightly pound with the flat side of a meat mallet to ½-inch thickness (see photo, right).
2 **tablespoons margarine *or* butter**	In a large skillet melt margarine or butter. Add pork to skillet and cook over medium-high heat for 4 minutes. Turn pork. Cook for 4 to 6 minutes more or till no pink remains. Transfer pork to a serving plate. Keep warm.

½ **cup whipping cream**	● Stir whipping cream, mushrooms, and calvados into drippings in skillet. Bring to boiling. Reduce heat. Simmer for 3 to 5 minutes or till slightly thickened. Pour sauce over pork. Makes 4 servings.
1 **2½-ounce can whole mushrooms, drained**	
2 **tablespoons calvados, apple jack, brandy, *or* apple juice**	

To pound the pork into ½-inch-thick pieces, place each piece between sheets of plastic wrap. Use the flat side of a meat mallet and strike lightly. The pork is tender so you won't need much force.

Skillet Meat-Loaf Dinner

Total Time: 40 minutes

1 **beaten egg** ¾ **cup soft bread crumbs** ¼ **cup milk** ¼ **teaspoon salt** ¼ **teaspoon dried thyme, crushed** ⅛ **teaspoon pepper** 1 **pound ground beef**	● In a medium mixing bowl combine egg, bread crumbs, milk, salt, thyme, and pepper. Add ground beef. Mix well. Shape meat mixture into 4 small loaves, about 3 inches long and 2 inches wide.
1 **8-ounce can tomato sauce**	● Preheat a large skillet over medium-high heat. Brown loaves on all sides. Drain fat from skillet. Spread the top of *each* loaf with about *one tablespoon* of the tomato sauce.
1 **cup beef broth** ¼ **teaspoon dried thyme, crushed**	● Add remaining tomato sauce, beef broth, and thyme to skillet. Bring to boiling. Reduce heat. Cover and simmer for 8 minutes.
1 **10-ounce package frozen brussels sprouts** 2 **cups frozen crinkle-cut carrots**	● Add brussels sprouts and carrots to skillet. Cover and cook 12 to 14 minutes more or till vegetables are crisp-tender and meat is no longer pink. Transfer meat loaves and vegetables to a platter.
2 **tablespoons water** 1 **tablespoon cornstarch**	● Combine water and cornstarch. Stir into tomato mixture in the skillet. Cook and stir till thickened and bubbly. Cook and stir for 2 minutes more. Spoon the sauce over meat loaves and vegetables. Makes 4 servings.

Small individual meat loaves cook faster than one large one, especially when you cook them in a skillet. Plus, serving is a breeze.

Total Time: 15 minutes

Snappy Ham Schnitzel

1 beaten egg
1 tablespoon water
1 12-ounce can (6 patties) ham patties
3 tablespoons all-purpose flour
⅔ cup fine dry seasoned bread crumbs

● Combine egg and water. Dip ham patties in flour, then in beaten egg mixture. Coat patties with bread crumbs.

You'll find canned ham patties on the refrigerator shelf with other canned ham products in your grocery store.

¼ cup margarine *or* butter
1 large tomato, cut into 6 slices
¾ cup shredded mozzarella cheese

● In a 12-inch skillet melt margarine or butter. Add patties and cook about 2 minutes on each side or till brown. Cut tomato slices in halves and place on top of patties. Sprinkle with cheese. Cover and cook about 2 minutes more or till cheese melts. Makes 6 servings.

French-Style Pork and Beans

Total Time: 25 minutes

½ **pound ground pork**
1 **large onion, chopped
    (1 cup)**
½ **teaspoon bottled minced
    garlic** *or* **1 clove garlic,
    minced**

● In a large saucepan cook pork, onion, and garlic till meat is brown and onion is tender. Drain off fat.

Both the Americans and the French have their favorite pork and bean dishes. In this version, we combined the flavors of a French cassoulet with American ingenuity.

½ **pound fully cooked Polish
    sausage** *or* **other
    smoked sausage**
2 **15-ounce cans great
    northern beans**
½ **cup dry white wine, beer,**
    or **beef broth**
½ **of a 6-ounce can (⅓ cup)
    tomato paste**
1 **bay leaf**
½ **teaspoon dried thyme,
    crushed**
⅛ **teaspoon pepper**

● Cut the sausage into ½-inch pieces. Stir sausage, *undrained* beans, wine, tomato paste, bay leaf, thyme, and pepper into the saucepan. Bring to boiling. Reduce heat. Cover and simmer for 10 to 15 minutes or till slightly thickened, stirring occasionally. Remove bay leaf. Makes 6 servings.

New England Sausage Dinner

Total Time: 35 minutes

3 **medium potatoes,
    quartered**
4 **medium carrots, cut into
    1-inch pieces**
1 **small head cabbage, cored
    and cut into 8 wedges**
1 **pound fully cooked Polish
    sausage** *or* **other
    smoked sausage**
2 **cups water**

● In a large saucepan combine potatoes, carrots, cabbage, sausage, and water. Bring to boiling. Reduce heat. Cover and simmer about 15 minutes or till the vegetables are tender. Transfer sausage and vegetables to a platter. Keep warm.

The classic corned beef and cabbage dinner simmers for at least 2½ hours. But, with fully cooked sausage, this close cousin is ready in a little more than half an hour.

1 **5½-ounce can apple
    juice**
1 **tablespoon cornstarch**
1½ **teaspoons dry mustard**
1 **teaspoon caraway seed**
¼ **teaspoon salt**
1 **tablespoon snipped
    parsley**

● For sauce, drain cooking liquid, reserving ½ cup. Return reserved liquid to saucepan. Stir in apple juice, cornstarch, mustard, caraway seed, and salt. Cook and stir till thickened and bubbly. Cook and stir 2 minutes more. Stir in parsley. Spoon sauce over sausage and vegetables. Serves 4.

Pork Medaillons with Apricots

Pork Medaillons With Apricots

Total Time: 20 minutes

1 **pound pork tenderloin**
1 **tablespoon margarine *or* butter**

● Cut pork tenderloin crosswise into 1-inch-thick slices. Season with salt and pepper. In a 12-inch skillet cook pork in margarine or butter over medium heat about 5 minutes or till brown on both sides, turning once.

1 **12-ounce can apricot nectar**
¼ **cup quartered dried apricots**
3 **green onions, sliced**
1 **teaspoon instant chicken bouillon granules**
¼ **teaspoon ground ginger**
2 **tablespoons water**
1 **tablespoon cornstarch**
Hot cooked noodles

● Add apricot nectar, apricots, green onions, chicken bouillon granules, and ginger. Bring mixture to boiling. Reduce heat. Cover and simmer about 5 minutes or till pork is no longer pink. Remove pork from skillet and keep warm.
  Meanwhile, combine water and cornstarch. Add cornstarch mixture to skillet. Cook and stir till thickened and bubbly. Cook and stir for 2 minutes more. Serve pork and apricot sauce over noodles. Makes 4 servings.

You *can* have it all. This tangy-sauced pork is quick to make, delicious, and elegant.

Beef with Marsala

Total Time: 25 minutes

2 **beef top loin steaks, cut 1 inch thick (about 1½ pounds total)**
3 **tablespoons margarine *or* butter**
1 **large onion, sliced and separated into rings (1 cup)**

● Cut steaks in half crosswise. In a 12-inch skillet melt the margarine or butter. Add the onion and cook over medium heat till tender, but not brown. Remove with a slotted spoon. Add steaks to skillet and cook for 5 minutes. Turn steaks. Cook to desired doneness (allow 5 to 7 minutes for medium doneness). Remove steaks from skillet. Keep warm.

½ **cup dry Marsala**
⅓ **cup water**
2 **tablespoons snipped parsley**
¼ **teaspoon salt**
⅛ **teaspoon pepper**

● For sauce, add the cooked onion, wine, water, parsley, salt, and pepper to drippings in skillet. Bring to boiling. Cook, uncovered, for 2 to 3 minutes or till slightly reduced, stirring to scrape brown bits from bottom of skillet. Remove from heat.

4 **slices French bread, cut ¾ inch thick and toasted**

● To serve, place a toasted bread slice on each of 4 dinner plates. Top each with a piece of steak. Spoon some of the sauce over each serving. Pass remaining sauce. Makes 4 servings.

Pictured on pages 4 and 5.

When you want to put your best food forward, bring out this exceptional dish—steak and onions served over toasted French bread and topped with a Marsala sauce.

Greek Tostadas

Total Time: 25 minutes

1 10-ounce package frozen chopped spinach	● Cook spinach according to package directions. Drain well, pressing out excess liquid. Keep warm.

We gave tostadas a Greek flavor with a lamb-yogurt filling and feta cheese.

¾ pound lean ground lamb *or* beef **½ teaspoon bottled minced garlic *or* ⅛ teaspoon garlic powder*** **1 teaspoon onion powder** **½ teaspoon dried basil, crushed** **¼ teaspoon salt** **⅛ teaspoon pepper** **½ cup plain yogurt** **2 ounces feta cheese, crumbled**	● In a large skillet cook lamb or beef, and bottled garlic till meat is brown. Drain fat from skillet. Stir in spinach, onion powder, basil, salt, and pepper. Stir in yogurt and cheese. Heat through but *do not boil*.

4 6-inch flour tortillas **1 small tomato, chopped** **2 ounces feta cheese, crumbled**	● Place tortillas on a baking sheet. Top each tortilla with one-fourth of the meat mixture, tomato, and cheese. Bake in a 400° oven about 8 minutes or till heated through. Makes 4 servings. ***Note:** If using garlic powder, add to the meat mixture with the spinach.

Enchilada Bake

Total Time: 30 minutes

½ **pound bulk chorizo *or* Italian sausage** ½ **cup enchilada sauce** ¼ **cup dairy sour cream**	● In a large skillet cook sausage till brown. Remove from heat. Drain fat from skillet. Stir in enchilada sauce and sour cream. Set aside.
2 **tablespoons cooking oil** 6 **6-inch corn tortillas**	● In a heavy medium skillet heat cooking oil. Dip tortillas, *one* at a time, in hot oil about 10 seconds or just till limp, adding more oil as necessary. Drain on paper towels.
½ **cup enchilada sauce** ½ **cup shredded cheddar *or* Monterey Jack cheese**	● Spoon some of the sausage mixture onto each tortilla, then roll up. Place filled tortillas, seam side down, in a 10x6x2-inch baking dish. Top with enchilada sauce. Cover with foil. Bake in a 350° oven for 15 to 20 minutes or till heated through. Sprinkle with cheese. Makes 3 servings.

Peppery and popular, Mexican cooking is hot in more ways than one. Try this speedy version of a favorite and see why.

SUPER FAST

Easy Tacos

Total Time: 20 minutes

8 **taco shells**	● Arrange taco shells on a baking sheet. Warm in a 300° oven while preparing meat mixture.
1 **pound bulk pork *or* Italian sausage** 1 **12-ounce jar thick and chunky salsa**	● In a large skillet cook sausage till brown. Drain fat from skillet. Stir in salsa. Heat through.
1 **cup shredded lettuce** ½ **cup shredded Monterey Jack *or* cheddar cheese**	● Spoon some of the meat mixture into each taco shell. Top with lettuce and cheese. Makes 4 servings.

Make it easy on yourself. To serve these tacos, set out the fixings and let everyone build their own.

Pork Chops With Rice

Total Time: 30 minutes

4 pork loin chops, cut
   1 inch thick
4 to 8 fresh basil leaves *or*
   ½ teaspoon dried basil,
   crushed

● Preheat the broiler. Cut a pocket in each pork chop by cutting a horizontal slit from the fat side almost to the bone. Sprinkle each pocket with salt and pepper. Place 1 or 2 basil leaves into each pocket or sprinkle pockets with dried basil.

A pocketful of fresh or dried basil flavors the pork chops.

1 4.5-ounce package regular
   chicken-flavored rice
   mix
1 6-ounce package frozen
   pea pods
1 tablespoon dry white wine

● Prepare rice mix according to package directions. Stir in pea pods and wine. Cook till heated through.

● Meanwhile, place chops on the rack of an unheated broiler pan. Broil chops 4 to 5 inches from the heat for 8 minutes. Turn chops. Broil for 8 to 10 minutes more or till meat is no longer pink. Serve rice with chops. Serves 4.

Sort-of-Swiss Steak

Total Time: 30 minutes

1 tablespoon cooking oil
4 beef cubed steaks

● In a large skillet heat cooking oil. Meanwhile, season beef with salt and pepper. Cook beef in hot oil over medium heat for 7 to 9 minutes or till brown on both sides, turning once. Transfer beef to a platter. Keep warm.

In this speedy facsimile of a classic dish, cubed steaks replace round steaks eliminating two time-consuming steps— pounding and simmering.

1 small onion, chopped
   (⅓ cup)
1 14½-ounce can stewed
   tomatoes
1 tablespoon
   Worcestershire sauce
2 tablespoons cold water
1 tablespoon all-purpose
   flour
   Hot cooked noodles
   or rice

● For sauce, cook onion in drippings in skillet till tender. Stir in *undrained* tomatoes and Worcestershire sauce. Combine water and flour. Stir into tomato mixture. Cook and stir till thickened and bubbly. Cook and stir for 1 minute more. Serve beef and sauce over noodles or rice. Makes 4 servings.

Index

T-Z

P

Q-S

Tips

Do you have any comments or
questions about this book? If
you do, we'd like to hear from
you. Please write:
Editor
Better Homes & Gardens® Books
1716 Locust Street
Des Moines, Iowa 50336